The Secret

Cosmic
Laws Within
Us

Dr Richard Allen PhD

"The universe will use any vehicle and any medium to communicate with us. Our job is to be alert and to listen."

— Elaine Seiler

The Secret

Cosmic Laws Within Us

Dr. Richard Allen, PhD
Revised Copyright MMXIII

Published in the United States of America.

Cover photo by Sharon Gail Legg 2011

PUBLISHED BY
SELF-IMPROVEMENT SUCCESS PUBLISHING
P.O. BOX 1246 - BOWLING GREEN, OHIO 43402 USA
www.NewLifeHypnosisCenter.com/self_help

DISCLAIMER AND TERMS OF USE AGREEMENT

The author and publisher have used their best efforts in preparing this book. The author and publisher make no representation or warranties with respect to the accuracy, applicability, fitness, or completeness of the contents of this book. The information contained in this book is strictly for educational purposes. Therefore, if you wish to apply ideas contained in this book, you are taking full responsibility for your actions.

EVERY EFFORT HAS BEEN MADE TO ACCURATELY REPRESENT THIS PRODUCT AND IT'S POTENTIAL. HOWEVER, THERE IS NO GUARANTEE THAT YOU WILL IMPROVE IN ANY WAY USING THE TECHNIQUES AND IDEAS IN THESE MATERIALS. EXAMPLES IN THESE MATERIALS ARE NOT TO BE INTERPRETED AS A PROMISE OR GUARANTEE OF ANYTHING. SELF-HELP AND IMPROVEMENT POTENTIAL IS ENTIRELY DEPENDENT ON THE PERSON USING OUR PRODUCT, IDEAS AND TECHNIQUES.

YOUR LEVEL OF IMPROVEMENT IN ATTAINING THE RESULTS CLAIMED IN OUR MATERIALS DEPENDS ON THE TIME YOU DEVOTE TO THE PROGRAM, IDEAS AND TECHNIQUES MENTIONED, KNOWLEDGE AND VARIOUS SKILLS. SINCE THESE FACTORS DIFFER ACCORDING TO INDIVIDUALS, WE CANNOT GUARANTEE YOUR SUCCESS OR IMPROVEMENT LEVEL. NOR ARE WE RESPONSIBLE FOR ANY OF YOUR ACTIONS.

MANY FACTORS WILL BE IMPORTANT IN DETERMINING YOUR ACTUAL RESULTS AND NO GUARANTEES ARE MADE THAT YOU WILL ACHIEVE RESULTS SIMILAR TO OURS OR ANYBODY ELSE'S, IN FACT NO GUARANTEES ARE MADE THAT YOU WILL ACHIEVE ANY RESULTS FROM OUR IDEAS AND TECHNIQUES IN OUR MATERIAL.

The author and publisher disclaim any warranties (express or implied), merchantability, or fitness for any particular purpose. The author and publisher shall in no event be held liable to any party for any direct, indirect, punitive, special, incidental or other consequential damages arising directly or indirectly from any use of this material, which is provided "as is", and without warranties.

As always, the advice of a competent professional should be sought.

The author and publisher do not warrant the performance, effectiveness or applicability of any sites listed or linked to in this book. All links are for information purposes only and are not warranted for content, accuracy or any other implied or explicit purpose.

TABLE OF CONTENTS

– Section Four –

THE COSMIC LAW OF GRATITUDE

– Section Five –

THE COSMIC LAW OF LOVE

–   Section Six –

THE COSMIC LAW OF ALLOWING

INTRODUCTION

"I've always hated the "Who are you?" question. This is a philosophical inquiry. Answering that question is why we're on earth. You can't answer it in thirty seconds or in an elevator."

— Sandy Nathan, Numenon

*I*n life, there are universal laws that govern

everything we do. And these universal laws never err, not even once. These laws are so perfect that if you were to align yourself with them, you could have so much prosperity that it would be coming out of your ears.

We all know the laws exist, but we really don't know much about them. We don't know what they are so we can get in tune with them. So we have to know what the universal laws are first, then everything else follows.

The first thing to consider when you try understanding the universe is to know who created the universe. Once you know this and why the universe exists, you'll gain a better idea as to why the universe is so powerful.

Now it depends on your belief system and what you were brought up to accept, because the creation of the universe was talked about in schools as having started with the Big Bang theory. This is where an explosion occurred and suddenly the universe appeared. Many scientists believe this theory because it is the easiest way to understand it. What they fail to understand or give credence to is who created the explosion to begin with. That mass of material that exploded just didn't appear there by itself. It had to have been created. This is why, no matter your religious beliefs, you must know that God is the one who created the universe for our use and to get whatever we want from it.

This God or Infinite Being as some prefer to call him creates everything in the universe in the image and likeness of him. This is why the universe is perfect. This is why it is powerful and dynamic. In order for everything to function in this capacity, God created laws that would automatically serve the purpose for what it was intended.

Whatever man wanted to do, if they worked in connection with these laws, would find plenty of abundance and perfection abounding, despite being sinful creatures themselves. The sin of humanity is not what fails in the person's life. It is failure to follow the universal laws that causes one to fail.

The laws that were created consist of the following:

- **Law of Gratitude: This is one universal law that states you must show gratitude for** what you have. If you show gratitude, you also show you appreciate the things in your life, no matter what those things may be. It is just a matter of acknowledging them and telling the universe that you are glad you have them in your life. By having gratitude, you actually speed your growth and success faster than you normally would. This is because if you appreciate the things you have, even if they are small things, you are telling the universe that you are accepting of them and you are open to receiving, and will receive more.

• Law of Attraction: Not many people know The Cosmic Law of attraction because they were never taught it. However, successful people know The Cosmic Law of attraction and practice it everyday. This is why they are successful. The Cosmic Law of attraction states that if you focus your attention on something long enough you will get it. It all starts in the mind. You think of something and when you think of it, you manifest that in your life. What you are doing is you think of what you want, which is the cause, and the effect is the object or person you manifest from your thoughts. For example, let's say you want $10,000, you think of receiving $10,000. You put an image of the money in your mind. This could be a mental picture of a check, or actual cash. But you think about it with an image. Now here is where The Cosmic Law of attraction comes in. When you dwell on this picture, you focus on it, and you put your emotions into it, the universe produces the results for you.

• Law of Karma: This law states that what you cause will have an effect. If you go out and do something bad, it will come back to you with something bad happening to you. If you do good for others, good things happen to you. By knowing this law, you will understand the power of the mind, and how your actions can speak for you in many ways good or bad. This power can hurt you or harm you, depending on how you use it. The principle here is to know you can create good or bad through your actions, because there will always be an effect no matter what.

• Law of Love: This is another universal law that God, or the universe, established for mankind. This happens to be the building block of all things. Love is more than emotion or feeling; it is energy. It has substance and can be felt. It takes on many forms. Love is also considered acceptance of oneself or others. This means that no matter what you do in life, if you do not approach or leave the situation out of love, it won't work. Everything in life is unified and by accepting this and working in harmony with it, you are working within the universal laws.

• Law of Allowing: This law states that in order for us to get what we want, we must be receptive to it. We just can't merely say to the Universe that we want something if we don't allow ourselves to receive it. This will defeat our purpose for wanting it in the first place. By working in harmony with this law, we are telling the Universe that we approve of ourselves getting what we want.

• **Law of Vibration: If you really want something, you wish on it, and you use your thoughts to visualize it, you are half way there to getting it. In order to complete the cycle you must use The Cosmic Law of Vibration to feel the part of what you want. You need to be in harmony with what you want, for it to work. Do this and you'll have anything you want.**

As you can see, there are universal laws and they were created for our good. To go in harmony with them will bring you peace and prosperity. But to go in opposition to them will bring you only despair and hatred.

Another factor you need to think about regarding the universal laws is that for everything to function properly there has to be structure. Without structure, our world or universe in fact, would be in utter chaos. If you study the laws and understand them, then cooperate with those laws, you will not only find yourself living in harmony with those laws, but your lives will be in tuned to the universe in such a way that you would have fulfilling, abundant lives filled with joy, peace, happiness, and good health.

If you examine successful people, you will find these traits. They understand the universal laws and apply them daily. They may not acknowledge that to you, but they do follow the laws. They do so in an intuitive way. But people who are not successful, those who struggle in life, are those who do not understand or embrace the universal laws. They may not understand what the universal laws are about because of the limiting beliefs they hold. As you grow to maturity, you are constantly taught beliefs by your parents, teachers, and even by your peers. These beliefs just placed in your conscious mind and eventually enter your subconscious where they are processed and acted upon. Once they are processed, they are stored in your memory banks for later retrieval. The only problem with non-successful people is that they don't understand these universal laws so they don't apply them in their lives. This is why their lives are full of anger, fear, and resentments,

instead of joy, peace, and contentment.

There is one truth that all people share to some degree or another. That is, there is a higher power and this higher power controls the universe and what we get out of it. The premise is that whatever happens does so for a reason.

And our higher power is what guides these events and allows them to happen.

Those people who know this, but wish to direct their own lives, follow the reasons and what results there from. They don't worry about what people do around them or blame others for their own mistakes or for being victimized. They know this can be a distraction and reframe from doing so. Instead, they take the time necessary to identify the cause, which allows them to see how they developed their present situation. It is at this time they can determine whether what they experience is desirable or not. If what they manifested was desirable, they would acknowledge it and repeat the process. This is a form of The Cosmic Law of Cause and Effect.

Successful people don't sit around and say "I'll try." No, they say yes they will do it. They have the "I will" attitude. This is important to accomplishing your goals of achieving what you want. People of this type aren't afraid to say no. They think the thought and take action to fulfill their thoughts. They believe in themselves and act on it. This is why success comes to them so quickly and easily.

Section One

The Cosmic Law of Attraction

Chapter One

"Start with big dreams and make life worth living."

- Stephen Richards

THE COSMIC LAW OF ATTRACTION

*T*he Cosmic Law of attraction is the most powerful

force in the universe. It is a law that if worked in harmony with, can bring you much in the way of blessings and success. If you work against it, it can only bring you pain and misery.

People who are successful know The Cosmic Law of attraction, but not many people know about it. This truth has been hidden for years. Very prominent people have kept it hidden from the lower class for many centuries only because some wanted all the fortune for themselves and did not want to share it. The outcome for these people was catastrophic. It is a known fact that if you knew The Cosmic Law of attraction, and acted in accordance with it, you could get anything you wanted in life.

Have you ever heard the old saying "like attracts like"? This is a law that means you attract what you are or vibrate to. So if you vibrate to goodness, goodness comes to you. Another way to look at this is by looking at yourself as energy. Everything in life is energy. Look under a microscope and you will see nothing but small atoms with space all around. And it is constantly moving. Nothing in this universe stands still. Atoms are constantly in motion. You can't see it but they are there and are in motion.

One form of energy attracts another form of energy. If you look at electrons, you will find one electron, which may be a weaker electron, is attracted to another electron. This is how electrons flow through wires.

The universal law of attraction is simple. We attract whatever we choose to give our attention to. It doesn't matter whether it is good or bad. If we focus on bad things, we will attract more bad things.

Ever heard of the expression everything happens in threes? The reason this happens is because when one bad thing happens, you are focusing on that bad thing so another bad thing or event occurs. As long as you focus on anything bad, badness will continue to manifest itself in your life. But the minute you stop focusing on bad and focus in on good, you change the pattern and now good things start coming your way.

It doesn't matter who you are or where you live. It doesn't even matter your religion or stature in life. The

Cosmic Law of attraction is there and works for everyone. You just have to connect to it.

Do you know you have enough energy in your body to light a city for a month? If you could tap into this, you wouldn't have to pay your electric bill anymore. But the only problem is we are conditioned not to use those resources for the betterment of ourselves. We allow others to control us, tell us what to think, say, or do. If we could harness the power of our minds, we would be invincible.

This is why for centuries, this law was kept secret from everyone. Imagine what you could achieve if you used one-tenth the power your mind possessed.

For years, we were brainwashed to follow a certain path. We couldn't think for ourselves. We had to just live day-by-day and solve problems as they came up. We couldn't use our creative mind to do the things we truly wanted to do. We were told that life was off limits and that we had to do what we were told or pay the consequences. Ever wonder why this world is so screwed up now? It is because we have been inhibited for so long. If we knew The Cosmic Law of attraction and applied it in our lives daily, we would have so much power and control that it would be scary.

When we live by others standards and just float along

from day to day, we are creating that type of world for ourselves. We are vibrating that way for ourselves. We are attracting that type of lifestyle, that type of way of living. But if we turned that around and started living the life we wanted, focused on the good things in life and really applied The Cosmic Law of attraction in every aspect of our lives, we would be superhuman creatures with the ability to command the world. We could literally have what we wanted, and when we wanted it. We would have total control of our lives.

In fact, if you are sitting down right now, think for a minute about a magnet. If you do not have one nearby, close your eyes and imagine one. Notice when you take a magnet and hold it close to metal, the metal is attracted to that magnet. What power right? That magnet literally grabbed and pulled that metal to itself. Imagine what you could do if you were like a magnet. But you know what? You are a magnet. Scientists have conducted much research on the brain and found there are neuro-transmitters in the brain that send signals from one stem and cell to another. These are electrical impulses that travel from the brain to the spinal cord, sending electrical impulses to the muscles in our body, forcing those muscles to move according to the way we want them. Because of this discovery, we have the ability to attract what we want by just using our mind. We attract because we have more power in our bodies than what the energy is outside of us. Therefore, if you use that power, you can do anything you want.

This is why when you think about scarcity, you get more scarcity. If you think about love, you get more love. If you think about abundance, you get more abundance. It happens. This is how The Cosmic Law of attraction works. And to work in contradiction to it can only prove fatal at most.

Therefore, if you think of yourself as a powerful attractor, and you use this God-given gift, you will attract more of what you want in your life, simply by thinking about it, then acting on it. However, there is one thing you need to know here. There is one ingredient you cannot leave out or The Cosmic Law of attraction won't work. You must not just think of what you want, you must also feel it. Put emotion behind it. Then when you put emotion behind it, take action by executing your desires and the actions you take will go out to the universe, which in turn will give you your results. It happens every time no matter what we think about.

Now someone may say, "I thought things come from our heart." Actually you are right. They do. Our heart is the seed of emotions. When we think of an object in our mind, we then send that image to our heart and act on it with emotion. This emotion we feel then forces us to take action. This is why, in a way, we do think from our heart. After we think of what we want from our mind, our heart takes over and sends out to the universe what we want and the universe responds. A formula makes this principle easy to follow. It is TFAR (Thoughts, Feelings, Actions, and Results).

If we want something in our lives, the first thing we do is think it. After we think it for a while (and this means placing images in our mind), we then transfer this to our heart, where we act on our thinking with feelings. Feelings we know are emotions. So when we feel something, we are using our emotions. After we have a deeply engrained feeling over the image or thought, we then act on that thought and feeling by taking action. When we take the necessary action, the universe shows up and gives us the results we wanted.

But we must act in harmony with it. We cannot just think, feel, and act only one time. We must live for the result every second of everyday. We must consciously and even subconsciously think about it every day. Like I said earlier, when you think and act on what you want, you must vibrate toward it for your desires to be fulfilled.

The Cosmic Law of attraction works by performing

three steps. And these steps must be done in order for the process to work. These steps are:

1.   Getting clear. You must know what it is you want or else you won't get it. The universe won't know what you are asking for, so how can it deliver.

Vibrate to the level of energy corresponding to what you want. If you want something and you think on it, feel it, and act on it, you must keep that level of energy going until you achieve the results you are after.

Attract what you want like a magnet. If you focus on what you want but don't allow it to come into your life, it won't. You have to be willing to accept it and acknowledge it. Then when you act, it will occur.

This whole idea of attraction does work. You just have to practice it every day. And since we are creatures of habit, when we get a hold on something and practice every day, we develop it into a habit. This then becomes automatic. The Cosmic Law of attraction can become the same thing. If you use it everyday, on a regular basis, and practice it this way, you will eventually, in a short period, find that it becomes a habit that you will subconsciously practice.

The Cosmic Law of attraction is working in your life right now but you may not be aware of it or notice it.

Whatever you do during the course of a day, whatever thoughts you think about, you are attracting. It is as simple as that. Think about it. You sometimes run across people in your life who tell you that something happened in their lives, something wonderful and they celebrate because they believe they attracted it. Do you know what I mean? But what about those people who seem to get what they refer to as bad luck. They always cry "Why me?" Why is this so? Because they attracted it. They vibrate to it, which caused it to happen. The first step to getting what you want is to own it or accept accountability for what you asked for.

Of course, there are those who ask why is it they ask for one thing, but still don't get it? This is because your vibrations or energy wasn't tuned into what you wanted. Remember, The Cosmic Law of attraction is you get what you think of. It has no distinction as to what is real or imagined. It doesn't know what is meant to be or not. It doesn't know whether you should have it or you shouldn't. It only responds to what you wish for and gives it to you.

How can you use The Cosmic Law of attraction? How can you practice it? What steps do you need to take to use it? You may not believe it, but the steps you need to take are easy. But you must do them, believe in them and believe in yourself, or they will not work. So are you ready to get tuned into the universe and get clear? Are you ready to work in harmony with the laws of the universe and become successful? If so here are the steps you need to follow:

1.   Get clear. You must know exactly what it is you want. If you are in doubt, vague, or too general, you won't get anywhere. You must know exactly what it is you want first. Only then will you be able to focus and concentrate on that thought.

Visualize what you want and vibrate to it. You must form a mental image in your mind so you can see it as if you had it in your possession. You must understand what it is you are seeing and look at it as if you can touch it. When you visualize it, you have to vibrate to it. Don't just see the image, feel it, touch it, let it become part of you. If it is a woman you want, visualize the woman you are looking for. Picture her hair color. See how tall she is. Notice her facial features. Visualize yourself holding her, hugging her, or even kissing her. Then transfer this image to your heart and use your feelings to convey how you feel about this woman. For women, you can do the same for a man. Repeat the same process, the only difference is you will be looking at a man instead of a woman. Regardless of your sexual preference, you just have to visualize the person in front of you and see him/her as being there with you and experience the joy of that person in your presence.

2.   Now allow it to be a part of you. You can allow it by simply agreeing to it and say yes to the idea that you want it. When you do this, you are in fact allowing it to come to you. If you visualize receiving a check for $1000, picture yourself accepting it while saying "yes" and "thank you." Hold it like it is yours. Embrace it. Tell the universe you acknowledge it and want it. Tell the universe "thank you for giving it to me" and then accept it. This way you are allowing it to come into your life.

Take action to fulfill your request. You must work in harmony with what you wish and do so without wavering. You must make a concerted effort to always dwell on wanting it. By doing so, you will attract it without any obstacles in your path. Remember, when you think, you then feel. After you feel, you take action. This action gives you your results. It works every time, no exceptions.

The above steps will help you to become better attractors. But you can also apply The Cosmic Law of attraction in your business life as well. How? Here are some ways you can use The Cosmic Law of attraction in your business dealings:

• **Identify your prospects: What you do here is simply list what you want in your ideal customer. Keep writing down everything you can think of that you want to see in the type of customer you want. Then think on this list in your mind.**

Vibrate on them: Instead of vibrating on the bad customers you may have gotten in the past, vibrate on those customers you want to see from the list you have written down and is now in your mind. Continue to vibrate and add feelings to the vibrations.

Follow through: When you start getting calls or making calls, and you have selected each client from those calls, celebrate that you have attained the client you were looking for. Keep doing this for each client that matched the list you made up. Pour your thoughts, emotions, feelings, and energy into that list and you will find the right clients will come knocking on your door, begging for your business.

Celebration time: After you have completed the list of clients and attained the amount of clients you want for now, celebrate the moment with acceptance. Look at yourself, give yourself a big hug, and say "I did it. I attracted these people. I am what made it possible to have these great clients. I created these clients with my intent. These clients came to me because of The Cosmic Law of attraction."

Get a bragging buddy: While you celebrate your success, find a buddy or friend who also celebrated attracting something or someone good in his or her life and celebrate together. Brag about it to each other. Acknowledge each other's achievements.

Keep a log: As you accomplish your goal and win new clients, keep a log of your success and how The Cosmic Law of Attraction worked in your life and present moment. Do this each time a new client comes on board. This way you can keep track of the methods you used so you can repeat them over and over again.

Review customer or client list: Every week review your client or customer list to see who you have on their and how many of them actually relate to your wants and desires. If you find a client or customer who doesn't match your requirements any longer, remove them and using the steps you used to create the original clients, put the process in motion and create more clients to replace the ones you removed.

When you use The Cosmic Law of Attraction, you do not worry about where it is coming from or how you will get it. The Universe will take care of those details. All you do is your part and the Universe will do its part. One important thing to mention here is that after you make your request, you cannot have any doubts as to your ability to get it. You must have strong assurance that you will get what you asked for no matter what. If you doubt for one moment that you don't deserve it, you cancel out your request and won't get anything. So, always focus on it and never have any doubts about what you ask for. The Universe is very giving. All you have to do is act in accordance with it, vibrate to it, and work along with it, and everything your heart desires will be yours.

The Cosmic Law of attraction is very powerful and forceful in the way it works. You can just think it, act on it, and bingo, it happens. But what would be even better is if you were to focus on an exact thing, event, or person you want in your thoughts. For example, let's say your goal is to marry a beautiful blond woman. You wouldn't just visualize any type of blond woman. You would visualize a blond woman with certain characteristics. You would want to visualize whether she wears glasses or not. You want to visualize the way she wears her hair. Is it straight or curly? Do you see the pattern? You want to be as specific as possible with your intent, or you may end up getting surprised and not get what you really want.

What if you wanted a certain amount of money? Visualize you getting a check for $10,000 dollars. Or maybe you want to go higher. Or perhaps you want to go lower? You know what you want. But you have to gear your mind so you can vibrate to it. Otherwise, if you aren't clear as to what you want, the universe won't know and will send you money that may not be enough for your needs. So think about that the next time you desire money in your life.

As was stated above; The Cosmic Law of attraction works. You just have to accept it, act on it, and be in harmony with it. Do this and you can have anything you want.

Chapter Two

"The tragedy is that what you disapprove of in others is the very thing you disapprove of in yourself."

— Stephen Richards

YOUR THOUGHTS CONTROL YOU

*D*id you know your thoughts control what happens

to you? That's right. There have been many books written on thought and how powerful it is. Thoughts do affect us in so many ways. Thoughts help us create the reality we experience. Whether that experience is good or bad, all of it is determined by our thoughts.

Thoughts create our emotional state. They affect our health. Thoughts even influence what we do and say to people. No matter what the situation or circumstances, everything we do stems from thought. Then the thought turns into feelings, which turn into actions, to finally results. There are actually three classes of thoughts we experience each day of our lives. These thoughts include positive, action, and worry.

We think each of these thoughts throughout the day.

If we have gratitude for who we are and what we achieve, we have positive thoughts. If we dwell on a future event that hasn't even happened, we have worry thoughts. And, if we think about what we need to do for the day, like going to the store or shop for a certain object, we have action thoughts.

Would you believe many of our thoughts are centered around worry? We aren't even aware of it at times but yet we do it. When we worry about something we have no control over, what we really have is fear turned inside. This is usually accompanied by some type of mental programming that tells us all the bad things that will happen before the event even started.

Some people think that if they don't worry, they can't prevent what will happen from occurring. They state that they are looking at the worst case scenario.

All types of worry are really just learned behavior that was acquired over time. And any thoughts that are learned can be unlearned very quickly. If you focus on positive thoughts instead of negative or worry thoughts, you would be surprised that your health would improve immensely. This is because positive thoughts create healing, and produce joy in our lives. Plus, positive thoughts reduce stress in our lives.

In order for you to be productive in life, you must

learn to control your thoughts. You must learn to use the right types of thoughts that enter your mind daily. Also remember that not all thoughts produce actions that lead to results. Only those thoughts that we dwell on predominately are what will lead to results for us.

Because our thoughts are powerful and can dictate what happens to us, we know we must control them. But what happens in situations when we start thinking negative thoughts? This happens to all of us from time to time. You may be in a very stressful situation and find you are thinking the worst case scenario instead of thinking positively. While you are thinking negatively, you start getting a lot of emotions over those thoughts. You begin to panic, your heart races. You start thinking of things imagined that could happen. You become irrational. What can you do in this situation? At this time you will need to stop yourself, remind yourself of The Cosmic Law of attraction, and get your thinking back on track.

A great way to stop the process of thinking negatively, and get your thoughts back to where they should be when experiencing something traumatic in your life, would be to stop and think out the situation. You don't know what will happen. You only know what has happened. So why are you getting all crazy over something that hasn't even happened yet? Evaluate your present thoughts and think of what your next thought will be. You will find that your next thought will probably take you into a more level headed feeling instead of outright lunatic. By thinking of your next thought, you will find your mind going away from the bad thoughts and you will quickly snap out of that thought pattern you are in.

As stated in this chapter, thoughts are dangerous, because they can lead you to get whatever you think. When you think, you vibrate to it; the universe receives your transmission and delivers. If you aren't careful, you may not like what you get back.

Chapter Three

"We are shaped by our thoughts; we become what we think. When the mind is pure, joy follows like a shadow that never leaves."

— Buddha

VISUALIZE YOUR THOUGHTS

*I*f you believe in The Cosmic Law of attraction, you

know that thoughts lead to feelings that lead to actions that lead to results. But you just don't think of a thought. You must visualize the thought as an image. For instance, let's say you want to buy a red convertible sports car. You visualize a red convertible sports car. But not just any sports car. It has to be a certain make and model. See this car in your mind and picture yourself in it, driving it, or having people in it. Put feelings and emotions into it. If you continue to do this, you will finally get that car.

It is easy to visualize. Believe it or not, we actually use visualization every day of our lives. When we daydream, we visualize. When we fantasize about something, we visualize. The thing about attraction is that we don't just visualize for one time, we practice it daily, maybe even two or three times a day, depending on how serious you want what you are visualizing about.

The only reason we haven't gotten anything from our visions

before was because we didn't have knowledge about the power of our visions.

If you look at people who are constantly in trouble or having bad things happening it is because they are always visualizing trouble in their lives. They are so used to doing it they don't know better. But for those who have success in their lives, they focus on the good stuff and continue to do that. They only visualize the good things coming to them. Visualization is used in all aspects of life from schoolwork to business. It has been silent for years only because of the unknown reason for it. Now even scientists are realizing the power of visualization.

The one good thing about visualization is it can be applied to any area of our lives and work every time. That is the power and flexibility of visualization.

Therefore, if you use visualization in your thinking and use your feelings and emotions to center that image, and then apply action to it, you will eventually see the results. Just try to focus on an exact image and not be too vague as to what you want. There have been people who have done general visualizations before and it has worked for them. They just trusted God or the Universe to surprise them with the results. So how do we perform visualization? The steps are not that complicated. You just have to perform certain routines and stick to them. Here are the steps you can take to help you visualize:

- **Sit in a relaxed position. Take a few deep breaths until you are completely relaxed.**

  After being fully relaxed, clear your mind of nothing.

  Next, picture the thing or event you want to happen. If you want a car, picture a car in front of you. But not just any car. Picture the exact car you want. Visualize every detail of the car from the front to the back, including the inside and how you want it to look. Do this until you have this image locked in your mind.

  Now, apply emotion to it. See yourself driving down the street, shifting gears as you go. Picture yourself stopping at a beautiful beach with the one you love sitting next to you.

  See yourself getting out of the car and taking the keys with you. Lock this complete vision in your mind and send it to your heart

for emotional processing.

If you apply the steps above each and everyday, you will find the car of your image appearing to you in some form or fashion.

No doubt, visualization is a very powerful tool, that can help you achieve the greatness, goals, or whatever you want in life, as long as you apply it to feelings and take action steps.

Section Two

The Cosmic Law of Vibration

Chapter Four

"It is your vibrational thoughts that give life to the goals you wish for."

- **Stephen Richards**

THE COSMIC LAW OF VIBRATION

*I*t has been said that in order for you to get what you

want you have to vibrate to it. How does this vibration work? In order to vibrate to something you must have positive thoughts. If you don't, you won't get what you are striving for.

When you are in a positive frame of mind, you will vibrate toward what you wish to achieve. If you have any slight negativity, worry, or are unsure in the slightest degree, this doubting or negative energy can inhibit you from accomplishing your task, unless you stop them immediately and focus on positive thoughts.

Let's say you are looking to get a million dollars. You visualize a check for that amount coming to you. The only problem is you have a slight doubt in your mind you will get it. What will happen? Nothing. You won't get it because you did not vibrate to it. You did not hold the belief that you would get it and did not have a positive attitude about it.

The premise here is that if you aren't sure you want something and you have slight doubts about it, you won't get it because you are not in vibration to it. You are focusing on what you do not want instead of on what you do want.

The Cosmic Law of Vibration starts that everything in life moves or vibrates. There is nothing that sits idle, even for a second. Everything in life is in a constant state of motion. Look in a microscope at an atom and you will see protons and electrons moving in a circle around a neutron. No matter what it is, it is energy and energy is in constant motion.

Everything that vibrates does so at a certain rate. This rate is known as its frequency. The higher the frequency, the more potent the force will be. Thought is considered the highest form of vibration therefore it has the highest frequency. Being the highest frequency, it is considered as a powerful force in the universe.

To understand The Cosmic Law of attraction correctly, and be in more harmony with it, we must also understand The Cosmic Law of Vibration.

The meaning of vibration can be considered as a moving backwards and forwards. It also can mean to oscillate, quiver, or swing. A perfect way to rationalize on this concept, think about this. If you stick your arm out straight and keep it perfectly still, you will notice no movement. You will notice your arm not moving, but what you don't realize is that under that skin of your arm, the electrons that are contained therein are moving on a steady basis. And they are moving at a speed of about 186,300 miles per second.

Although the arm appears still, it really is in a constant state of motion. You can't see this happening because your eyes can't pick up such minute particles of matter. You can only see this happening if you had a powerful microscope to view it.

Now take a second and vibrate or shake your arm around. Your arm was already vibrating on its own, but you have stepped up the vibration or assisted it to become stronger. The vibrating energy of your arm has increased dramatically.

Those who think positively are in a good state of vibration. Because they are in a good or positive state of vibration, good things will always come to them. They will always attract positive things or personalities. But those thinking negative would be vibrating negative energy. This is because they dwell on the bad and all that is pessimistic. As such, they will vibrate negativity. And because they vibrate negativity, they will attract anything negative in their lives. This means they will attract trouble, anguish, fear, rage, or whatever negative emotion is available.

If you want to control the results you get, you must control what you vibrate to. This means controlling your thoughts because you only vibrate to the thoughts you have. If you don't get what you want in your life, this is because you are ignorant of what you want. Or you are ignorant to The Cosmic Law of Vibration. In electronics (if you know electronics – if not just play along), there are electromagnetic fields. If there are two electromagnetic fields working together, they are working in harmony or in resonance. When this occurs, the vibrating rate can easily be transferred from one to the other by way of electrons. The best way to describe this is by providing an example. Let's say you have a glass sitting on a table. There is a lady singing nearby. She hits a certain high note that cracks the glass; but no other note cracked that glass. Only that one frequency cracked it because the two frequencies were in resonance. The frequency of the lady's voice was the same as the frequency of the magnetic field surrounding the glass. See my point?

The same thing happens to your thoughts. When you think of something, and vibrate to it, you are creating a frequency. That frequency goes out into the universe and reaches an object that also vibrates at that same frequency. When this happens, the two are in synch. The electromagnetic waves your brain creates from your thoughts vibrate to the exact energy level as the thing or object that is in the universe you ask for. By concentrating on these though patterns, you increase the energy level of those thoughts and therefore the thoughts become more potent.

Remember when you practice The Cosmic Law of attraction; you must inculcate The Cosmic Law of Vibration. The two go hand in hand. There is no separation of the two. When you practice one, you also practice the other.

Section Three

The Cosmic Law of Karma

Chapter Five

"Like success, failure is many things to many people· With Positive Mental Attitude, failure is a learning experience, a rung on the ladder, a plateau at which to get your thoughts in order and prepare to try again·"

— W. Clement Stone

WHAT IS COSMIC KARMA?

*A*ccording to the Buddhist teachings, The Cosmic

Law of karma says that for everything you do there is a result. Or as they say, for every cause there is an effect. This effect could be good or bad, depending on the cause.

Therefore, what The Cosmic Law of karma is telling us is that we all are responsible for our actions in some form or fashion. What we do or the actions we take will result in some form of result.

An example of this could be if we do a good deed for someone; the effect is kindness from the person receiving the good deed. Another example is that if we think bad thoughts of someone, our thinking will reflect in our actions, which will result in us either doing harm to that person, or saying something bad, which could result in hurt feels or resentment later.

But if we dwell on good, enhancing thoughts, we will only have the best of intentions and will treat the person, who is the center of our thoughts, with good will, hopefully resulting in a return of kindness of some type.

If the thoughts we have for someone else never materialized to the person (the person was not available to receive the actions), what would happen in turn is that those thoughts would turn into feelings, but inward instead of outward. Therefore, these thoughts would stay buried deep inside ourselves until either we find a release somehow or we find the person the original thoughts were for, and give off those thoughts, whether good or bad. This would clear us of our thoughts, but the end result or effect could still be disastrous for the other person.

In order to live in peace and harmony with ourselves and the universe, we must live with positive energy, not negative. For every action, there is an equal and opposite reaction. This goes along with the Biblical text that states, "we sow what we reap". Therefore, what we produce or cause to occur we will get a result or effect.

The Cosmic Law of karma tells us that if we live in a body-consciousness, we are not pure in karma. For this level of consciousness only produces sexual lust, anger, greed, ego, and other negative emotions. Instead, we have to be linked with the Supreme Soul to have true karma, peace and harmony.

Chapter Six

"Our life is what our thoughts make it."

— **Marcus Aurelius**

UNDERSTANDING COSMIC KARMA

Based on the previous chapter, The Cosmic Law of karma relates to cause and effect. But some people believe it relates to fate or predestination. However, this is not the case. Karma means action. It means to do something, but the action specified here is not mechanical action. It is not unconscious or involuntary action. It is an intentional, conscious, deliberate, willful action. How is this possible? It is because every action must, no matter what, have a reaction.

So, based on The Cosmic Law of karma, when we do an act that is intentional, we reap the results or effect, either good or bad. Thereby, if we do an act of kindness, the effect or result will be some kind of kindness.

There are occasions where there is a delayed result. If this happens we don't know if the action is wholesome or unwholesome, at least till the result has been satisfied. Until then the cause can be wholesome momentarily until the result appears, at which the cause may now be changed to an unwholesome cause instead.

According to karma, there are three doors of action. These three doors are body, speech, and mind. If we break these down into groups, we have three unwholesome actions we must avoid for each group. When we start with body, the three actions we must avoid are killing, stealing, and sexual misconduct. As for speech, we must avoid four unwholesome actions. These are lying, slander, harsh speech, and malicious gossip. In the final group, which is mind, there are three unwholesome actions to avoid. These are greed, anger, and delusion.

If you avoid all ten unwholesome actions, you will avoid the consequences that result from doing them. The reason you need to avoid the unwholesome actions is that they only cause suffering for those who are at the recipients of the actions.

This is why those who do bad things continue to do bad things. In their minds, this is all they know. The root cause of their badness is in the thoughts they have for themselves and the way they carry themselves.

Whereas, those who are good and upright people, and practice this on an everyday basis, always have good coming back to them.

The old saying "what goes around comes around" is very true. This is also part of the laws of attraction and karma. To accept these laws, you accept the universal laws as set up by the Supreme Ruler of the Universe. Act in harmony with them and you will do well; act against them and you will suffer.

Section Four

THE COSMIC LAW OF

GRATITUDE

Chapter Seven

"Great men are they who see that spiritual is stronger than any material force - that thoughts rule the world"
                                        - Ralph Waldo Emerson

THE COSMIC LAW OF GRATITUDE

*A*re you grateful for what you have in your life? Do

you acknowledge that every day when you wake up in the morning? You should. Do you know that The Cosmic Law of attraction includes The Cosmic Law of Gratitude?

By having The Cosmic Law of Gratitude, you believe firmly that the Universe or God, depending how you view it, is there to give you what you want when you ask for it, that you deserve what you get. You relate to what you have and act in accord to it.

People who lack gratitude always seem to find themselves living in poverty or not having the lifestyle they wish to have. They look upon themselves as lower than anything else and wonder why they can't be better than what they are. The primary reason for this is that they lack acceptance to what they want and do not show to the Universe what they want or deserve to have.

There is no doubt that you get what you ask for and you get it in abundance when you put a lot of effort into it. By showing gratitude, you are showing that the effort you put forth was in tune to what you desired; and you will obtain more of that you wish.

You can tell people by what they have and by what they get just by seeing them and looking at how they dress, walk, and act. You can usually tell if they have gratitude by the way they present themselves.

This is why when you look at rich people, you notice they get richer. They have a debt of gratitude and show it every day. This way, they are telling the universe that they are glad they have all these riches and deserve them. The universe responds by giving them more.

If a person does have abundance but does not show gratitude, he will eventually lose it. This is because he is telling the universe that he does not deserve it. When the universe perceives this, the universe stops delivering.

On the other hand, if a person lacks abundance but shows gratitude for what he has, the universe will see that and will in turn give the person more of what that person wishes. This way, that person does not stay in lack for very long.

If a person lacks abundance and does not show gratitude, he will continue to live with lack because he has not shown he deserve more.

This is why when we show gratitude, we are closer to God or the Universe than anyone else. And we get the rewards for doing so. Therefore, the more grateful we are when we get good things, the more good things we will receive. And in some cases, these good things will start coming more rapidly than before. As you create new thoughts and act in harmony with those thoughts with a show of gratitude for having those thoughts, the closer you will be to getting that of which you thought or ask for.

Gratitude has many benefits in that it can keep you from feeling inadequate. It can keep your mind focused on the good rather than the bad. You can think more abundantly by having gratitude. This is why you must obey The Cosmic Law of Gratitude if you want what you seek.

Think about this. If your show of gratitude is strong, the results that come back to you will be strong. If your debt of gratitude is continuous, your supply will also be continuous. If you start losing your attitude of gratitude, you will find you will lose ground rapidly and end up on the losing end of life. This is why having gratitude is so important. It is so important that it was made into one of the universal laws.

If you think about it, without gratitude, there is a

missing link somewhere in our lives. We know that something should be there, but may not realize it until someone points it out. The fact is that saying, "thank you" for what you get is a big step toward having a form of gratitude. But this isn't all there is about The Cosmic Law of Gratitude. In fact, there is a good definition of The Cosmic Law of Gratitude that states, "If you are to get the results you seek, it is imperative that you should act on and obey this law." This means that if you do not obey The Cosmic Law of Gratitude, you will not get what you seek. It is that simple.

Other than being grateful for what you have, what is the exact way that The Cosmic Law of Gratitude works? It can be stated as a natural principle that action and reaction are equal and opposite in direction at all times. This means that whatever we put our attention or emotional energy on can be good or bad. And this energy will eventually show up in our lives. This is one of the principles you must know and understand. Neither the universe nor our subconscious mind knows good or bad. Both aspects are treated the same. In this regard, what we put our focus on is what we get back.

The importance here is on putting positive energy out to the universe. This way, we are focusing on what we want not on what we don't want. You may not realize this, but gratitude is very powerful. It has a lot of high-energy positive vibration of thought. This is why I mentioned above that having gratitude connects you to the Universe or God, depending on how you look at it.

Without gratitude, you have no power, since the two connect together. And by using our minds for positive things, we are in reality using the power we have to produce the reality we want. So when we show gratitude, we are in fact producing high energy positive vibrations of thought. This high energy can only lead to one manifestation – great achievements.

When you do anything in life, you put forth the gratitude to make it work. If you set goals for yourself, you must show gratitude for having accomplished the goals you put down. When you do write your goals down, think of them as having been already achieved and be grateful for them being achieved. Your gratitude will be so powerful, so energized, that people around you can't help but notice that about you.

Those who are not successful or do not get what they want are in fact pushing away the success and are violating the universal law of gratitude. In fact, there are five key mistakes or ways of thinking that people make with gratitude that cause them not to get what they want in life. These five ways include:

1.   **Abundance: Some people wonder if there is enough to go around for everyone. If your belief that the universe has only a limited supply, you are going nowhere in life and will never amount to anything. This is a major fallacy in life. In fact, there is more than enough abundance in the universe. It is endless. God promised us that we would have abundance forever if we chose to have it. The universe is energy. Energy is everlasting. Therefore, what we want comes from energy. It only goes to show that the universe will never run out of anything we want. It will always supply us with what we want when we want it. We just have to ask.**

Non-resistance to what is: This is a mistaken thought or principle that people have. It keeps us from having the gratitude we should have. When we think with non-resistance, we are in fact having the mental attitude that whatever happens, happens. We don't fight it, we just let it be. In other words, people who think this way believe they deserve what they got or believe that was the way it was supposed to be. Therefore, they limit themselves to what life has to offer. If it involves something they can't do anything about, they just let it be and state that is the way it was meant to be. In this case, you can apply The Cosmic Law of opposites and think that there is good in the situation instead of bad.

No satisfaction: People tend to associate satisfaction with being happy and having abundance. But there is a difference. When you are satisfied, you accept what is. You can be satisfied without being grateful. This is because you accepted things the way they are and not challenge it. Happiness, on the other hand, is a state of joy or gratitude. It is a very positive and attractive mental energy. By being satisfied, you are actually limiting yourself to what you can have in your life. It is important to be happy and satisfied now. It you do, you will have gratitude and will be in the position for much abundance.

Forgiveness: You may not know this but forgiveness is also a part of The Cosmic Law of Gratitude. This means you need to forgive anyone who did bad things to you in the past and even in the present, as well as in the future. This is especially true if you have a grudge against someone for a long time. The way you know you forgive them is by asking yourself if you can either wish them well or be grateful for them. If you can truthfully answer "yes," you have indeed forgiven them. Forgiveness is so vital to our dreams in life that if we don't do it and hold any resentment, fear, or any frustration inside, it can literally block us from getting what we want in life. Lastly, we must learn to forgive ourselves for what we do to others and our own selves. If we can look at ourselves in the mirror and say we love ourselves, we are on our way to experiencing the life we want.

Stop thinking: Unfortunately, people want to stop thinking after they get a thought in their head. They don't want to go beyond thinking and act on what they think. They go into the steps of thinking, but they never act on what they think. Therefore, the key to having gratitude is by acting out what you think. What better way to act than to give of yourself or your time to help others?

Obeying The Cosmic Law of Gratitude is part of and includes The Cosmic Law of attraction. If you want success in your life as well as abundance, you will obey these laws and when you do, you can get whatever you want in life and be happy doing it.

Section Five

THE COSMIC LAW COSMIC LOVE

Chapter Eight

"Always aim at complete harmony of thought and word and deed. Always aim at purifying your thoughts and everything will be well."

— Mahatma Gandhi

THE COSMIC LAW OF LOVE

*L*ove is another universal law that we must adhere

to. In the beginning of time God showed his love by creating Adam and Eve. He then later showed his love by allowing his son Jesus to come to earth to die for our sins. That was the greatest show of love of all time. God also showed love when he created man, and in his likeness. Therefore, humans are capable of showing and receiving love.

There are different levels of love that God created. But the one main feature of The Cosmic Law of Love is that if we give love, we get love back. This is true in many cases. If we fall in love with someone, they in turn fall in love with us. When we fall in love, we don't expect them to love us in return, although we would like them to. No, we love them for who they are.

We can show we are in turned into this law of the universe by simply doing the following:

- **Recognize and accept that we are love as created by God.**

Show love to others. Be gentle and show respect to others in the way we speak, think, and in our actions.

Don't let your ego get in the way of loving others. Treat the ones closet to you with dignity and respect. Above all else, show love to them. Don't let any issues interfere in your love with your closet companion.

Always be centered and connected with your inner being or spirit, whichever you prefer to call it.

When you love others, do so unconditionally. Do not accept or expect love in return. Love others as they grow in spirit and in personal growth.

Keep your lines of communication open with your inner self and with others. And do not forsake the thought or idea to display love to others.

The above points really sum up The Cosmic Law of Love. Actually, life itself shows God's love. If we embrace it, grow with it, and get connected to it, we can have plenty of abundance in our lives. Even The Cosmic Law of Love goes to The Cosmic Law of attraction. God's love for humanity is so strong that he is willing to give us what we ask for. We just have to ask in love and accept it when it comes to us.

Section Six

THE COSMIC LAW OF ALLOWING

Chapter Nine

"What matters is to live in the present, live now, for every moment is now. It is your thoughts and acts of the moment that create your future. The outline of your future path already exists, for you created its pattern by your past.

— Sai Baba

THE COSMIC LAW OF ALLOWING

*Y*ou just thought about something you wanted. You

have used The Cosmic Law of Attraction, The Cosmic Law of Vibration, and all the other Universal laws to request what you want. Now you need to complete the cycle and use The Cosmic Law of Allowing to permeate your very being, which will in turn accomplish the feat you set out and will achieve what you wished on from the beginning.

Think about this fact. Everything in the universe is composed of energy, as you probably are already aware. This energy works in cycles. If you studied electronics, you will understand this more fully. Basically, AC or alternating current is composed of a cycle of electrons that start from zero or neutral, goes into the positive cycle, then dips down into the negative part of the cycle, then it comes back to neutral again. This is the way energy works as well. It is in a constant cycle or vibration.

If you wish to complete the process of the Laws of the Universe, you must use The Cosmic Law of Allowing to complete the cycle of Attraction. This is where the cycle of energy comes in. When you use your thoughts to manifest something in your life, you are in fact telling the universe what you want. You put feelings and emotions into it. You vibrate to it. It becomes a part of you. Every ounce of your very being is tuned into it. Now, to complete the cycle of energy flow, you must complete the circuit by allowing the results to occur for you. You must intent it to come to you unrestricted.

This is why some people seem to get what they want while others do not. The people, who do get what they want, use all the Laws of the Universe in precisely the right way. They are not only tuned into their own thoughts and feelings, but they feel it in their soul. They vibrate to it and they acknowledge it as already being a part of them. They send out the signal to the universe that they are one with what they want and are claiming that they are allowing themselves to receive it without doubt, fear, or worry. This, my friends, is what you need to do if you want to get what you want.

The Cosmic Law of Allowing will work for you if you let it. What you must agree on is that you are worthy to receive your gift. That you are worthy to receive the prize you are after.

The problem with this world is there are just too many instances of anti this or anti that. People are constantly pushing things away. They are saying no to drugs, no to smoking, no to this or no to that. They are saying no to war, no to violence, and no to everything else. What people don't seem to realize is that The Cosmic Law of attraction states that what you think about or wish for you will receive. If you think about war, you'll see more war. If you think about drugs, you'll see more drugs. The fact is, you are allowing these things into your life, and this is why you are seeing it.

No wonder people are constantly complaining that they don't have anything. They can't make ends meet. They can't get ahead in life. They can't do this. They can't do that. For every "can't" there is another creation that is born. If you say you can't afford this because you don't have enough money, you are telling the universe in fact that you don't have any money. Well guess what? The universe hears you and obeys. Your wish is my command and you get what you wish for. You are allowing poverty in your life and this is why you don't have abundance.

So how can you change this? How can you reverse this and become more abundant in your life? The answer is to simply ask for it. You have to think about what you want, not what you don't want. If you wish for more money, ask for it. Don't go around saying you can't afford something. You are telling the universe that you can't afford it. Therefore, you won't get the money you want. But if you switch that around and tell the universe that you do want it, that you do have the money, the universe will respond and give it to you. It is that simple.

The bottom line here is that you must remember to use all the Laws of the Universe if you expect to get what you want. You must complete the cycle of energy in order to complete the circuit between you and the universe. You are the power source and the universe is the component part of the circuit. The path will flow but it will stop with the universe if you do not have a complete path for the energy to return. This means you must use The Cosmic Law of Allowing to accept what you wish for. This will complete the path back to you and you will receive what you wished for. You in fact, sent your energy to the component, and the component responded by turning on. It then sent the energy back to you to complete the circuit and to tell you everything is working on all cylinders.

This is the way The Cosmic Law of Allowing works. If you work in harmony with it, focus your energy the right way, and tell the universe you want it and are ready to receive it, you will get it.

The best way to practice The Cosmic Law of Allowing is by simply saying "yes" to things you receive in your life. If someone says something nice to you, say "thanks." You are telling the person you are allowing his comments to be received. If someone gives you a gift, say "thanks." You are telling the universe and the person that you are allowing yourself to receive the gift. You need to do this with everything in life that you want to receive. Of course, if you don't want something, you politely say "no" to it. But be careful here. What you say "no" to may benefit you in the long run later. So be sure that you think about it before you say "no." In one form or fashion, you just may need that situation or product or whatever it is you are saying "no" to.

To fully understand The Cosmic Law of Allowing, you have to look at it from the standpoint of resistance. If you resist something, you will not get it. That is as simple an explanation as you can have. When you use The Cosmic Law of Allowing, you are saying that you have no resistance to what you want and the flow of energy will be easy and direct. There will be no stumbling blocks.

Summary

"Man, alone, has the power to transform his thoughts into physical reality; man, alone, can dream and make his dreams come true."

— **Napoleon Hill**

The basic premise with The Cosmic Law of

attraction, Law of Vibration, Law of Gratitude, Law of Love, and Law of Allowing, is that when you practice these laws, and stay in harmony with them, you will prosper. You will have abundance. You will have plenty.

There is no denying it. Your thoughts control your actions. Your thoughts dictate what you end up getting from the Universe. If you believe completely that you will receive what you wish for, good things will come your way. You must accept that which you wish upon. You must be tuned into the universe to get it. You must be in vibration to what you want. You must show the universe you want it by having gratitude for what you have received. You also must show that you are allowing it by being receptive to it and saying "yes" to it when it comes. By doing this, the universe will manifest it to reality and provide you more.

The main point with this book is to draw your attention to the fact that there are universal laws God put in place to help us. He loves us and wants the best for us. By acting in harmony with his will and by obeying his universal laws, you will have plenty. You just have to start the process with a thought, turn that thought in an image, send it to your heart for processing (this turns into emotions and feelings), act on your thoughts, and allow the results to come to you. By doing this you will receive results from your thoughts, whether they are good or bad.

The old saying is, "be careful what you ask for" or "you are your thoughts" holds true in Cosmic Laws in every respect. Watch your thoughts, if you want the best that life has to offer put the Secrets of the Cosmic Laws to work in your life. Practice them daily and you will see abundance work throughout the Universe through the inner God.

The Egyptian Winged Globe

"And to YOU who are in fear of my name the sun of righteousness will certainly shine forth, with healing in his wings; and YOU will actually go forth and paw the ground like fattened calves."
(Malachi 4:2, NWT)

Why have we used The Winged Sun Globe or Disk throughout this book? The Winged Sun Globe is from Egyptian mythology, it represents the symbol of the metaphysical trinity of the holy spirit, which flies, as it were, through the mind (air) from the higher nature (heaven) to the lower nature (earth) and soars aloft to the self (sun).

The wings carry us to spiritual protection and bring forth courage through strength and prayers, wisdom through spirit, and bring forth knowledge of spirit filled mystical magic from within. The wings give us the ability to see hidden spiritual truths, illumination, healing and creation. The wings lift us to the sun to see the material and the spirit of the inner God that flows through us.

About The Author:

Rev· Richard Allen, PhD

Dr. Allen has had a lifelong interest in metaphysics and the paranormal along with psychology and a particular interest in hypnosis and self- hypnotic techniques to expand the mind and attune oneself with the Inner God. His spiritual belief system is that of a Christian Meta-physician.

Originally from Columbus, Ohio he has traveled extensively, speaking and giving demonstrational workshops on many educational and spiritual subjects.

After a life time of study he obtained his Doctorate from the University of Sedona, located in Sedona, AZ.

Dr. Allen is well respected by his pears and has clients from around the world who purchase his books and attend his self-help seminars, both in-person and virtually worldwide through internet technology.

Dr. Allen is a skilled hypnotist, and numerologist, certified by the National Guild of Hypnotist in 1994. He is also a member of the New York Virtual Chapter of the National Speakers Association.

For more information, updates and other books and audios in this series or for information on online webinars, seminars and workshops conducted by Dr. Allen, Please contact him through the publisher:

SELF-IMPROVEMENT SUCCESS PUBLISHING
P.O. BOX 1246 - BOWLING GREEN, OHIO 43402 USA
www.NewLifeHypnosisCenter.com/self_help

You can follow Richard "Rick" Allen on Facebook:

facebook.com/NumerologyExpert

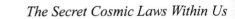

The Secret Cosmic Laws Within Us

-BONUS BOOK CHAPTER-

Here is a bonus chapter from, **Creative Visualization: The Key to Getting What You Want in Life**. one of the many books in the Self-Improvement Publishing series. If you would like more information on obtaining this, and other books or audios in this series contact the publisher today.

Chapter Nine

WHAT IS AN EMOTIONAL GUIDANCE SYSTEM?

......and how will it spur the process of turning my thoughts into reality?

The emotional guidance system is an illustration which helps you understand what you are thinking and consequently, feeling strongly about.

You know that thoughts cause feelings, right? Read the headlines on the papers and if you saturate yourself with articles reporting about terrorist activities, genocide, hate crimes, poor political will or government inefficiencies, you will feel depressed, angry and desperate.

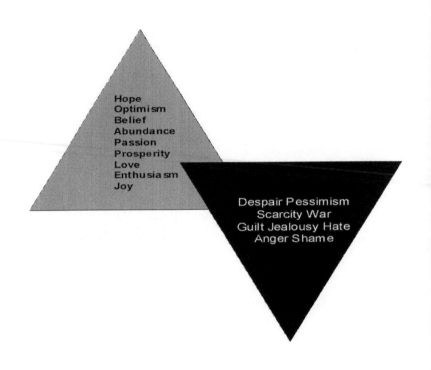

Hope
Optimism
Belief
Abundance
Passion
Prosperity
Love
Enthusiasm
Joy

Despair Pessimism
Scarcity War
Guilt Jealousy Hate
Anger Shame

The Emotional Guidance Illustration

On the other hand, if you surround yourself with good news like astounding human interest stories, inspiring real-life tales and amazing feats or discoveries, you will be upbeat, projecting a certain glow sure to be noticed by people around you.

What the emotional guidance system does is to

classify your feelings into two categories: the good and the bad. As you can see in the illustration, good feelings include hope, belief, abundance, prosperity, passion, love, enthusiasm and joy. The bad feelings, on the other hand, are comprised of despair, pessimism, fear, guilt, jealousy, hatred, anger and shame. Knowing your feelings will help you act in a way that is in alignment with your desired goal.

In the case above of the good and bad newspaper articles, what do you think should be done? Of course, this doesn't mean that you have to disregard the negative news and focus solely on the good news. What you should do is to celebrate the worthy write-ups and spread them to other people. Like a pebble being tossed into a pond, this will create a ripple effect and many lives will be blessed with the knowledge of such good and wonderful news. For the bad news, consider taking positive action. Instead of lamenting about the war on terrorism, support peace campaigns. Enjoin others to participate in inter-faith dialogues to promote harmonious coexistence. Encourage your friends and relatives to attend interracial meetings to break down the barrier of animosity and suspicion. Do not allow stereotypes to hinder you from reaching your goals. Break it down with the power of visualization and positive gestures.

Always find ways to be in or around a positive force. If possible, be the source of positive feelings yourself. Start a gratitude journal. At the end of the day, list all the things that you are thankful for, no matter how trivial they may seem. If somebody offered you a cup of coffee in the workplace, or a friend dropped by unexpectedly just to say hi, or a neighbor volunteered to take your beloved Dalmatian for a walk, be grateful. You do not need earth-shattering miracles to jolt you into a thanksgiving mode. Little acts of kindness are what really matters.

You can also help out at a local charity. Leading a fund-raising committee, helping out at a local soup kitchen, putting your hobbies to good use – all these contribute to the attraction of positive vibrations towards you. Do good.

The universe merely corresponds to the nature of your inner feelings.

Always remember this: **What you think, what you feel and what manifests are always a match.**

Life can be absolutely phenomenal, and it should be.